Analyze It!

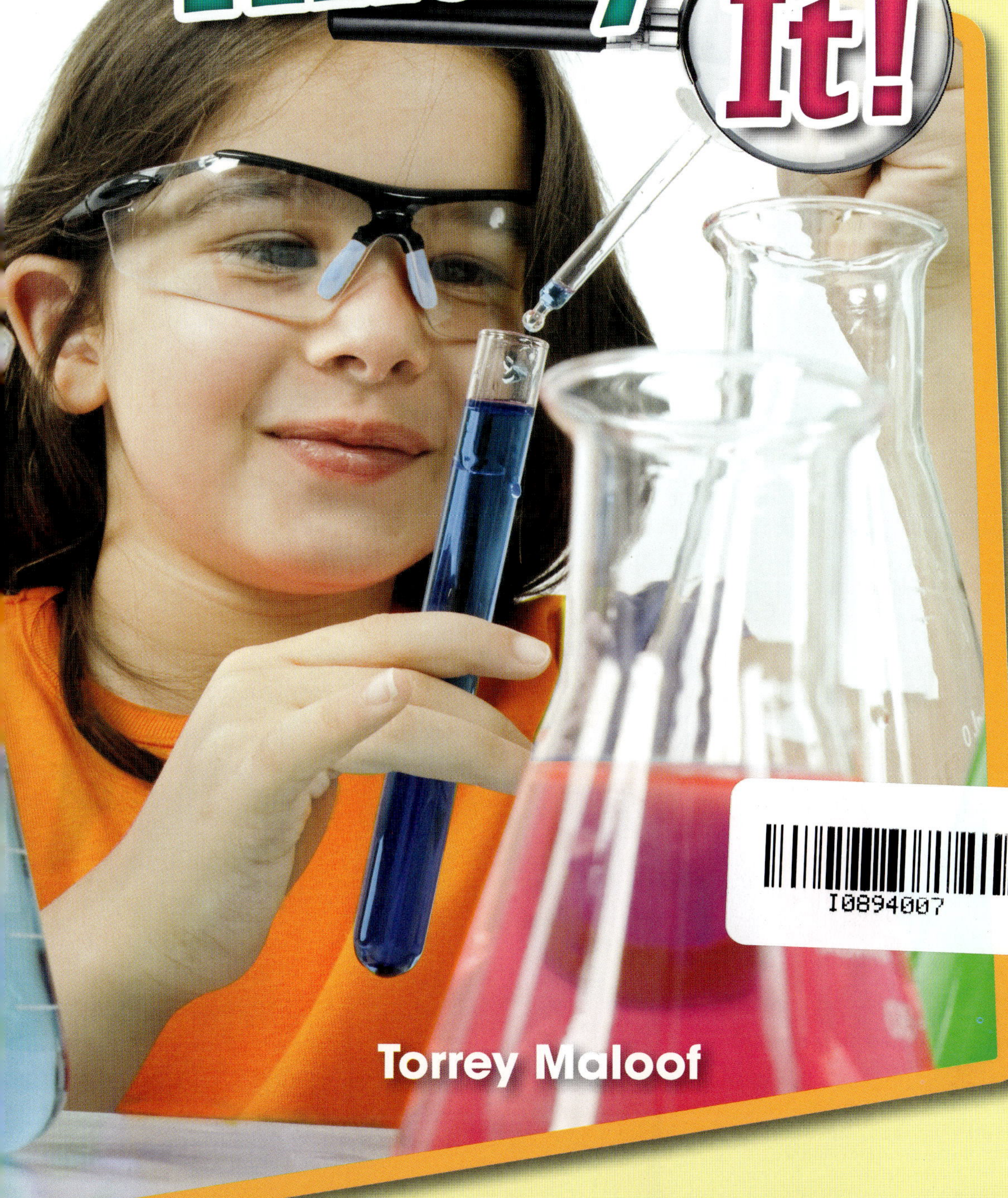

Torrey Maloof

I0894007

Consultants

Sally Creel, Ed.D.
Curriculum Consultant

Leann Iacuone, M.A.T., NBCT, ATC
Riverside Unified School District

Image Credits: p.19 (right) Huntstock/age fotostock; p.14 (bottom) marco scataglini/age fotostock; p.27 (top) Blend Images/Alamy; p.26 Blue Jean Images/Alamy; p.21 (left) Cultura Creative/Alamy; p.12 GFC Collection/Alamy; p.9 Juice Images/Alamy; p.22 (left) Martin Shields/Alamy; p.32 OJO Images Ltd/Alamy; p.23 Frontiersin.org; pp.10–11 xefstock/Getty Images; pp.6, 7 (top), 8 iStock; pp.18–19 LOC_AGBell/Library of Congress; p.22 (right) NATGEO; p.4 World History Archive/Newscom; p.5 (both) Science Source; p.24 ER Degginger/Science Source; p.17 Health Protection Agency/Science Source; p.16 USGS; pp.28–29 J.J. Rudisill (illustrations); all other images from Shutterstock.

Teacher Created Materials
5301 Oceanus Drive
Huntington Beach, CA 92649-1030
http://www.tcmpub.com

ISBN 978-1-4807-4613-8
© 2015 Teacher Created Materials, Inc.
Printed in China
Nordica.082019.CA21901100

Table of Contents

Big Questions

Is Earth flat? Is it really in the center of the universe? What makes people ill? How can an illness be cured? Why do objects fall toward Earth? Why do they fall at the same speed even if they are not the same size?

These are all questions that have been asked and answered by scientists.

Marie Curie studies chemicals in 1912.

Scientists are **curious**. They ask many questions. They want to study and learn about the world around them. They take their work seriously. Scientists work carefully to find answers to their questions. Then, they share those answers with the world.

Question It!

Kids can be scientists, too! Think of a question that you want to answer, and use science to answer it.

Alexander Fleming studies bacteria in 1928.

Isaac Newton studies color and light in 1666.

How It Works

Science is all about facts. Scientists can say if something is true or false. And they can prove it! They do this by using the scientific **method**. This is a set of steps that can help scientists answer questions.

Scientists always start with a question. This is the first step in the scientific method. Scientists want to know why or how something works. When they know what they want to study, they think of a question.

Next, they may do **research** to find answers. Scientists read books on the topic. They may use the Internet. They find as much helpful information as they can.

Research It!

When you have a question, do some research! Be sure to take good notes. Record everything you learn about your topic.

A scientist tests a hypothesis about plants.

The next thing scientists often do is form a **hypothesis** (hahy-POTH-uh-sis). This is what scientists believe is the right answer to their question. It's their best guess. Scientists put a lot of time and effort into this guess. They do a lot of thinking. They look over their research closely. They use the research to help them form their hypothesis.

A good hypothesis is one that can be tested. That is often the next step in the process. Scientists have to prove whether their guess is right or wrong. This is where the real fun begins!

Write It!

When you have a question, think about what the best answer may be. This is your hypothesis. Remember, your hypothesis must be one that can be tested.

Test It!

When you think of a scientist doing an **experiment**, what do you see? Do you see a science lab? Are beakers bubbling? Is smoke rising out of test tubes? Is a scientist someone with crazy hair wearing safety goggles? The truth is, there are many ways to do an experiment. And they don't all look the same.

Think It Through!

When you have a hypothesis, think of the best way to find out if it is true. Then, test it!

Experiments are tests. Scientists do these tests to learn more about things. This is how they prove whether a hypothesis is right. First, they choose what to test and how to test it.

Scientists must use their five senses when doing a test. The senses are ways we take in information. They are taste, smell, touch, sight, and hearing. Scientists look closely with their eyes. They listen carefully with their ears. But most of the time, the five senses are not enough. Scientists need to use more tools.

Before scientists do a test, they gather their supplies. The tools they need vary for each test. It depends on what is being studied.

This scientist gathers supplies before studying mice in South Africa.

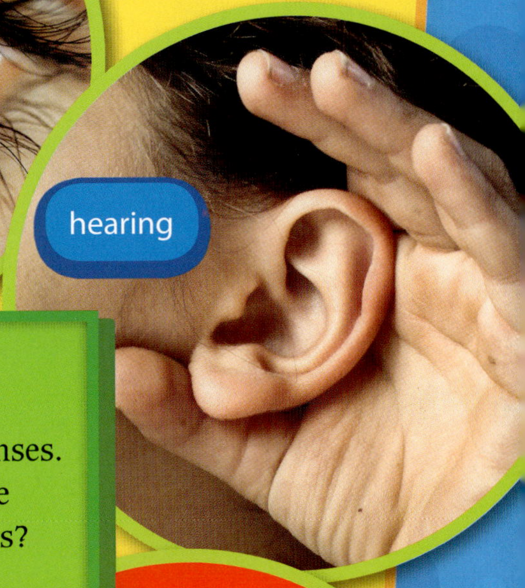

Sense It!

Think about the five senses. Which ones will you use during your experiments?

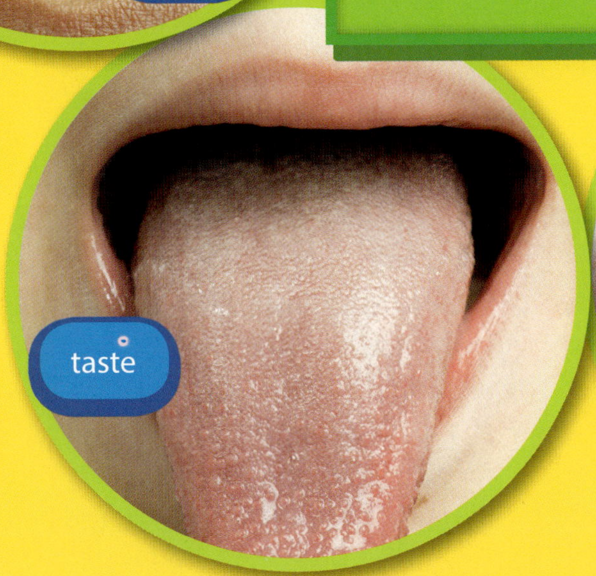

List It!

Make a list of all the tools you will need for your experiments.

A telescope is a tool that some scientists use to study space.

Scientists use many fancy tools. If they are studying stars, they may need a telescope. This is a tool that helps them see far into space. If scientists are studying something such as small bugs, they will need different tools. They may need a microscope. This makes small objects look bigger.

Scientists use many basic tools. They may use things such as watches or timers. They may use measuring cups or rulers. They may use a camera to take pictures. The tools that scientists use are endless!

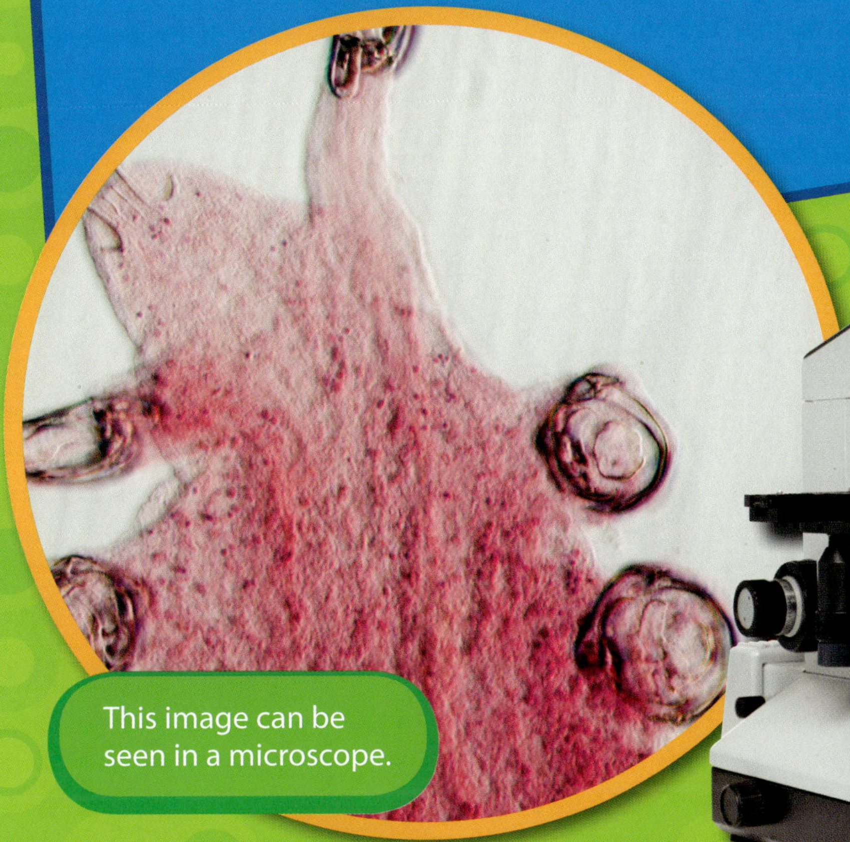

This image can be seen in a microscope.

Once scientists have their supplies, it is time to list the steps and do the test! Scientists list all the steps they will take before they do the test. They do this so that they won't forget steps or make mistakes. They also do this so other scientists can do the test, too. This is important. Scientists do not know if a hypothesis is true until many people test it and prove it.

These scientists study a volcano.

Scientists are very careful when they do tests. They may wear a lab coat to protect their skin. Or they may wear goggles to protect their eyes.

Be Safe!

Make sure you have an adult help you with your experiments. And make sure you have all the safety gear you need!

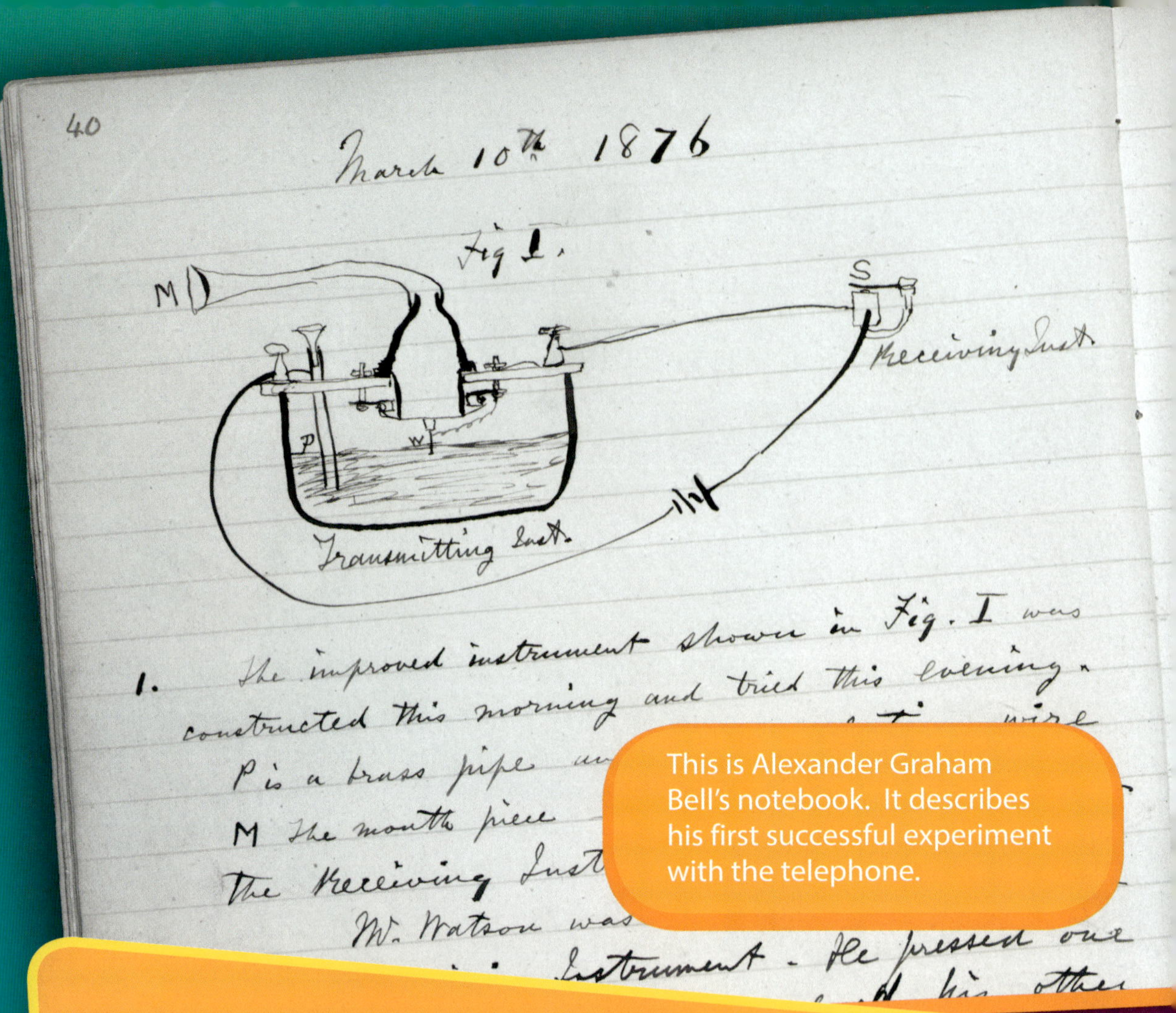

This is Alexander Graham Bell's notebook. It describes his first successful experiment with the telephone.

Record and Analyze It!

Scientists take notes during their tests. They record everything! They make sure to include a lot of details. They may draw pictures. They may draw charts or graphs. They collect **data**. Data are the facts they find while doing the test. Scientists may enter the data in a computer.

you". To my delight he ca
t he had heard and understood
I asked him to repeat the word
answered "You said 'Mr. Watson
out to see you.'"
ees and I listened at S w
d a few passages from a boo
uth piece M. It was
t articulate sounds procede
et was loud but indistinct
If I had read beforehand
Mr. Watson I should h
ery word. As it wa
ake out the sense — bu
ord here and there wa
made "to" and "out
the sen

Organize It!

Think about how you will organize your data so it's easy to read and makes sense to others.

Scientists need to keep their data neat and organized. This is so other scientists can read the data. It helps them **analyze** (AN-l-ahyz) the data, too. This is the next step!

What does it mean to analyze data? It means thinking about all the facts. Scientists look at the data very closely. They look for patterns. They look for connections. Then, they make a **conclusion**. This means they look to see whether the hypothesis is right.

Scientists are not always right. A lot of the time, a hypothesis is proven wrong. And that's okay! This is a key part of the process. Even if scientists are wrong, they still learn from the tests. Now, they can form a new hypothesis and do more tests!

Analyze It!

Take time to think about your data. What do you notice? Was your hypothesis correct? How can you tell?

Share It!

The last step in the scientific method is to share the **results**! Scientists don't do a test just once. They do the same test many times. If they get the same results each time, then they share the information with other scientists. They share the list of items they used. They share the steps they took. They share the data they collected. And they share their conclusions.

You can learn about scientists' discoveries in many science magazines.

Next, other scientists perform the same test. If they get the same results, then the information is shared with the world!

You can review scientists' discoveries on websites like this one.

Tell It!

Tell a friend about your experiments. Share all your information. Have your friend do the same experiments. See if your friend gets the same results.

Scientists have made some cool discoveries lately. They made these discoveries by using the scientific method. For instance, one day, you may have an invisibility cloak, just like Harry Potter. Yes, really! Scientists have found a way to make small objects disappear. They do this by bending light.

This machine bends light.

Another discovery is the zombie ant. They are real! First, a fungus grows in an ant. (A fungus is something that eats away at dead plants and animals.) The fungus takes over the ant's brain. Next, the fungus makes the ant find it a new home. Then, the ant dies. How crazy is that?

What cool science discovery will you make?

zombie ant

Scientists study the brains of animals to learn more about the human brain.

Think Like a Scientist

Scientists never stop thinking! They ask questions and seek answers. They are always learning. They spend much of their time studying. They do research. They do tests. They analyze data. Scientists work hard to help us better understand our world.

Question

Think Big!

Research

If we knew what it was we were doing, it would not be called research, would it?

—Scientist
Albert Einstein

Some experiments are simple. Some experiments are complex. Some only have a few steps. Some have lots. There are some tests that require many materials. Others use very few. But all scientists use the scientific method. And anyone who uses this method can be a scientist!

Let's Do Science!

How can you use the scientific method to learn about plants? See for yourself!

What to Get

- a cup half-filled with water
- knife
- red food coloring
- stalks of celery with leaves

What to Do

1. Add a few drops of food coloring to the cup of water.

2. Have an adult use the knife to cut off the bottoms of the celery stalks. Place a few stalks of celery in the water.

3. Now, closely observe the celery over the next few days. Remember to take detailed notes and draw pictures.

4. After a few days, remove the celery. Break it into pieces. Study the celery closely. What do you see? Analyze your data. Draw a conclusion. Retest. Then, share your findings with friends.

Glossary

analyze—to study something closely and carefully

conclusion—knowledge that is formed after much thought and research

curious—having a desire to learn or know more about something

data—facts or information used to analyze something

experiment—a scientific test in which a series of actions are performed and observed to learn about something

hypothesis—an idea that can be tested

method—a way of doing something

research—careful study that is done to gain new knowledge about something

results—something that is caused by something else that happened or was done before

Index

Your Turn!

My Experiment

Pretend you are a famous scientist. You have access to the coolest scientific tools in the world. What would you study? What would you test? What would you prove, and how? Write a paragraph and draw pictures about your experiment.